TRADITIONAL TALES
from
INDIA

Vic Parker

Based on myths and legends retold by
Philip Ardagh

Illustrated by
Nilesh Mistry

Thameside Press

Distributed in the United States by
Smart Apple Media
1980 Lookout Drive
North Mankato, MN 56003

Editor: Stephanie Turnbull
Designer: Zoë Quayle
Educational consultant: Margaret Bellwood

Library of Congress Cataloging-in-Publication Data

Parker, Vic.
    India / written by Vic Parker.
        p. cm. -- (Traditional tales from around the world)
    Summary: A collection of stories taken from the various
cultures of India.
    ISBN 1-930643-38-1
    1. Tales--India. 2. Legends--India. [1. Folklore--India. 2.
Mythology, India.] I. Title.

PZ8.1.P2234 In 2001
398.2'0954--dc21
                                                        2001023216

Printed in Hong Kong

9 8 7 6 5 4 3 2 1

CONTENTS

INDIAN TALES

**The stories in this book were first told hundreds
of years ago in India. India is a huge country.
It was once made up of many small kingdoms.
These included the places we now call Afghanistan,
Bangladesh, Bhutan, Nepal, Pakistan, and Sri Lanka.**

Long ago India was a place of dry deserts as well as snowy
mountains, thick rainforests and golden beaches. Wonderful
animals roamed the land, including tigers, snakes and elephants.
Wealthy kings ruled from splendid palaces over many different
peoples. Some people were warriors, others were farmers.
They all had their own customs, beliefs, and holy men.

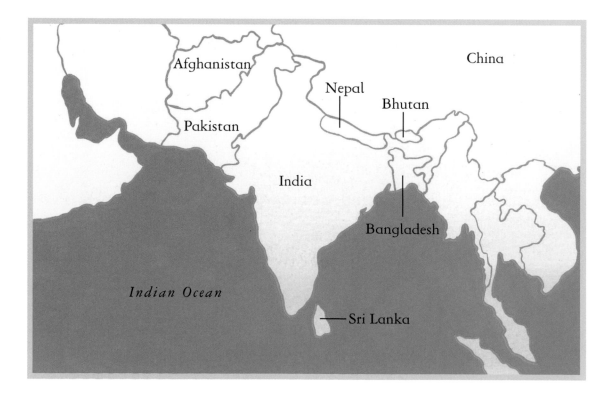

**The first Indian stories to be written down
were told about four thousand years ago.
The tales were about the ancient gods
and formed the basis of the Vedic faith.**

As time passed, a new faith called Hinduism gradually took over. It had new gods such as Vishnu. Hindus believe that they live not just one life but several. This idea is called reincarnation.

Reincarnation is also an important part of Buddhism, which began in the sixth and seventh centuries BC and follows the teachings of Buddha. At the same time, Muslims came to settle in India. Muslims believe in just one god, as do the Sikhs, whose religion began much later, in the sixteenth century AD.

In this book you can read traditional tales from all these different faiths, retold in new ways for you to enjoy.

*Krishna, a Hindu god, is often shown as a fun-loving
young man who enjoys dancing and playing the flute.*

THE LORD
OF DEATH

Deep beneath the earth lay the underground kingdom
of Yama, the lord of death. Whenever people died, their
spirits were brought down to Yama. He decided whether
they should go to one of the heavens or stay in his
kingdom for punishment. Yama was not a fearsome
god—at least, not for people who had led good lives.
Yama ruled for justice, not evil, and he was always
a fair judge.

The lord of death often left his kingdom of the dead
and went traveling through the sunny land of humans.
On one trip, Yama saw a beautiful woman and fell in
love with her at once. He disguised himself as a human
and asked the woman to marry him. To his delight
she accepted.

The newlywed couple lived together very happily.
Of course, Yama's wife had no idea that her husband
was really the mighty lord of death.

Soon Yama's wife gave birth to a baby son.

"We'll call him Yama-Kumar!" sighed Yama happily,
as he cuddled the little one.

"Why on earth do you want to name him after the lord of death?" asked his startled wife.

"We'll call him Yama-Kumar," smiled Yama, "and that's final!"

It was the last time that Yama got his own way in anything. From that moment on, things changed. Yama's wife had set ideas about how the baby should be brought up, and she became very bossy. The lord of death wasn't used to being ordered around, but he loved his wife and tried to put up with it.

As the child grew older, things became worse. Yama was nagged, nagged, nagged all the time. Finally, he couldn't take it anymore. One day Yama simply disappeared back to his kingdom—but he didn't forget his son. He kept a close watch over the boy as he grew into a young man.

One night, Yama appeared to his sleeping son in a dream.

"I have something important to tell you," Yama said. "I am the lord of death, but I am also your father. My son, I would like to give you a very special present. Work hard to become a doctor, and the gift of healing will be yours."

Yama-Kumar woke with a heart full of excitement.

Day after day, he worked hard to understand all about injuries and illnesses. Week after week, he studied how to make medicines from herbs, plants, and insects. The young man qualified as a doctor in half the usual time.

The lord of death was delighted.

"I am very proud of you, my clever son," he said to Yama-Kumar in another dream. "I am going to do something else for you. Every time you visit a sick patient, I will appear to you at their bedside—even though no one else will see me. If I nod my head, you will be able to cure the patient with your skills. If I shake my head, the patient will surely die."

Yama-Kumar quickly became known as the greatest doctor in all the land. If Yama-Kumar said he could make a patient better, the person would always recover, no matter how ill they might have been. On the other hand, if Yama-Kumar said there was no hope for a patient, no doctor in the world could make the person well again.

Years passed, and Yama-Kumar was called to the royal palace itself. The king and queen were beside themselves with misery, as their beloved daughter lay sick and dying. They had tried all the royal doctors, but not one had been able to help. Now Yama-Kumar was their only hope.

As Yama-Kumar was shown into the princess's room, he saw his father's shadowy shape appear next to her bed. The lord of death grimly shook his head and raised his noose, ready to catch the princess's soul. Yama-Kumar listened to the wailing of the king and queen outside the door and looked down at the girl's lovely face.

"No, Father!" he suddenly cried. "Please let the princess live! She is young and beautiful, and her parents love her deeply."

The lord of death looked into his son's eyes.

"The princess can live for three more days," he sighed. "But that is all."

After that, Yama-Kumar didn't leave the princess's bedside—not even to eat or drink. He sat and cared for her and thought hard. All the while, the sound of sobbing echoed through the sad, still palace.

One day passed . . . then a second . . . then the third . . . and the lord of death silently appeared again.

"It is time," the god commanded.

Yama-Kumar's heart began to beat faster.

"Father," he said bravely, "allow the princess to live until she's at least a hundred, or I will tell my mother who you really are and where she can find you."

The lord of death froze. What a terrible thought!

It would be nag, nag, nag, forever and ever. In his own kingdom, too. There would be no escape!

"Very well, my son," the lord of death sighed. He lowered his noose. "It's a hard bargain, but don't breathe a word to your mother!" With that, he vanished.

It took several days for Yama-Kumar to heal the princess with his herbs and medicines. At last she was back to normal, laughing and happy. The king and queen were so delighted that they insisted the princess marry the wise, young doctor. Yama-Kumar and his lovely bride lived happily to a ripe old age, just as the lord of death had promised.

THE STORY OF RAMA AND SITA

The great god Vishnu watched over the balance between good and evil on Earth. Whenever Vishnu saw that there was too much wickedness in the world, he went down to Earth and put things right.

Once, Vishnu became very worried about a terrifying demon called Ravana, who had ten heads and twenty arms. The evil Ravana had tricked another god, the lord of creation, into giving him special powers of protection. Now no god or demon could harm Ravana and he was free to do whatever evil he wanted. Vishnu decided that something had to be done, so he was born on Earth as a prince called Rama....

One day, the demon Ravana was feasting in his throne room when his sister burst in, screaming. Her nose and ears were gone and the wounds were oozing blood.

"Who has done this to you, sister?" Ravana roared, leaping to his feet.

"I fell in love with a handsome prince called Rama," the demoness wailed, "but he was already married!

13

He would have nothing to do with me. I tried to kill his wife, but Rama's brother, Lakshman, found me and attacked me!"

The cruel demon threw back his ten heads and laughed. "You got what you deserved!" he bellowed.

His sister groaned, "That is not all. Our brother went to take revenge for my wounds, but Rama killed him and all his warriors!"

Ravana howled with rage, and the palace walls shook.

"I couldn't help falling in love with Rama," his sister moaned. "He is so brave and fearless and his wife, Sita, is even more beautiful than Rama is handsome! I'm sure if you saw her, you'd want to hold her in your arms."

The demon's eyes glittered cruelly.

"I shall have revenge on these feeble humans, Rama and Lakshman, and take Sita for myself!" he bellowed.

Ravana sprang outside and leaped into his magic chariot. He cracked his whip, and the chariot flew off the ground and raced into the clouds....

Meanwhile, Rama was enjoying a walk in the forest with his beautiful wife, Sita, and his brave brother, Lakshman. It was a sunny day and all was peaceful.

Suddenly Sita glimpsed a flash of gold through the trees, and she stopped still.

"Look, it's a golden deer!" she gasped. "How wonderful! Oh Rama, please catch it for me. I'd like it as a pet."

Lakshman looked worried.

"I have never seen a golden deer before," he said. "Be careful, brother. It may be a demon trick."

Rama thought quickly as the golden deer trotted away.

"Lakshman, you must look after Sita while I'm hunting," he decided. To be even safer, Rama drew a magic circle around his wife. "Whatever happens, Sita, do not step out of this ring," he said. Rama kissed Sita and was gone like a shadow into the undergrowth.

Lakshman and Sita waited in the sunshine. Leaves rustled overhead. Flowers nodded happily in the breeze. All at once, they heard a cry of pain in the distance, and Rama's voice called out,

"Lakshman! Sita! I am hurt...."

The startled pair turned to each other in alarm.

"Stay inside the magic circle," Lakshman urged, and he dashed away to help Rama.

Unfortunately, Lakshman's fears were true. Everything was part of a wicked plot by Ravana. The golden deer was one of Ravana's demon followers in disguise. It had lured Rama away on purpose, then it had cried out in Rama's voice so that Lakshman would leave Sita, too.

All the time, Ravana was hiding nearby. As soon as the demon saw that Sita was alone, he turned himself into a wrinkled old holy man and hobbled up to her. Sita was so anxious about Rama that she barely glanced at the old man.

"Pretty one," the disguised Ravana croaked, "why do you pay me no respect?"

The worried Sita had forgotten the custom of giving holy men food and drink.

"I'm so sorry!" she blushed. Without thinking, she stepped out of the magic circle to find something to offer.

With a roar of glee, the demon changed into his true monstrous form. In a flash, he grabbed Sita. He tied her to his chariot and they raced away like the wind, leaving the forest far below.

This all happened so fast that only the king of the birds, a vulture, spotted the terrified Sita being carried away. The huge bird bravely threw himself in front of the chariot to try to stop it. The heartless demon slashed off one of the noble bird's wings and laughed as the bird king plummeted through the skies. The sobbing Sita began to drop her jewels, hoping that they might leave a trail for Rama to follow....

Ravana was triumphant when he reached his palace.

What he didn't know was that the dying bird king had managed to tell Rama what had happened. The heartbroken Rama followed Sita's trail of jewels. He gathered an army of monkeys and bears, and they attacked the demon in his own palace.

Ravana was furious, but he was sure that no one could hurt him. He was wrong. The brave Rama killed the demon with a single arrow. Ravana hadn't realized that he was only protected from other gods and demons, not humans!

The god Vishnu's work was done. He had rid the world of the terrible demon, and good and evil were balanced once more.

KRISHNA AND THE DEMON KING

The god Vishnu looked down and saw that wickedness was about to overcome the world once more. A demon king had seized control of a kingdom in northern India. This demon's magic was so strong that even the gods trembled to think of all the evil he could do. Only Vishnu had the power to stop the demon king. He would have to visit Earth as a human once again....

The demon king soon found out by magic that Vishnu was planning to be born as the son of a certain nobleman. The demon king wasn't worried. When the nobleman's wife gave birth to a baby boy, the demon king simply murdered it . . . and the second . . . and the third . . . and the fourth . . . and the fifth . . . and the sixth. The bloodthirsty demon king enjoyed killing each tiny boy more than the last. He was sure he was going to stop Vishnu from being born on Earth.

But none of these babies was the god Vishnu.

The nobleman and his wife were deeply distressed by the killing of their six sons. When they found out they were going to have a seventh baby, they wept with fear.

Luckily, the gods magically took the baby from the noblewoman and gave it to a woman who lived in a faraway village. The baby was another boy, who was named Balarama.

The delighted nobleman spread a lie that the child had died. When the heartless demon heard the news, he thought that death had cheated him of another enjoyable murder. He was furious!

Soon he heard that the couple were expecting another child. He was determined that *this* time he would have the pleasure of killing the baby himself. He ordered soldiers to guard the noblewoman's chamber night and day.

Imagine the noble couple's terror when their eighth son was born! They expected the demon king's guards to burst in at any second and seize little Krishna—for that was what they called him. The panicking couple huddled together, hugging their son tightly. Without any warning, their tiny baby suddenly turned into the great Vishnu before their very eyes.

"Do not be afraid," the god commanded. "Take me to the village where my brother Balarama is living safely. A woman there has just had a baby girl. Give me to her and take her child as your own. The demon king is only interested in your sons, so he won't harm a girl."

As the image of Vishnu faded, so did the couple's memory of their vision. They were left with no idea of what had just happened or who their newborn son really was, but Vishnu's escape plan was still clear in their minds. As the couple wondered how they would open the locked chamber door, it sprang open. Outside, the guards were asleep and snoring, every single one!

The nobleman and his wife didn't wait to find out how this had happened. Clutching their beloved son, they ran away as fast as they could.

The fearful couple didn't stop running until they reached the wide, rushing River Yamuna. The nobleman took a deep breath, lifted baby Krishna high above his head, and strode straight into the swirling, white foam. In only two steps, the water was racing around his waist. Two steps more and the icy wetness covered his chest. Two more steps and all that could be seen of the nobleman's head was his hair, eyes, and nose.

The determined father swayed and staggered as the strong current tried to sweep him off his feet. The racing waters began to splash Krishna, and the baby stretched out his tiny, chubby arm. Suddenly there was an ear-splitting WHOOSH! and the river divided in two, leaving a dry path across the riverbed.

Shaking, the stunned nobleman dashed for the far bank. He hurried to the village, and the babies were exchanged. Krishna was safe.

Eventually, the demon king found out he had been tricked. He was so furious that he ordered all the baby boys in his kingdom to be put to death instantly. Then the demon king tried everything in his power to kill Krishna, from poisons to whirlwinds. None of it worked. Krishna had the wisdom, strength, and skill of the mighty god Vishnu himself, and he foiled the demon king's evil plans every time.

Finally, when Krishna had grown into a young man, the demon king sent word that he wanted to make peace. He asked Krishna and his brother Balarama to come to a wonderful festival at his palace.

Of course, the warm invitation was a trick, but Krishna and Balarama were ready for anything. As soon as the brave warriors drew near the demon's palace, an enormous, wild elephant was sent to attack them. The ferocious beast charged at Krishna, but Balarama leaped forward and hit the elephant so hard that he killed it with just one punch.

As the brothers arrived at the city gates, a huge, hairy wrestler came out and challenged Krishna to a fight.

The wrestler had never lost a fight in his life, but Krishna threw him to the ground in seconds.

At last, Krishna strode right up to the demon king's throne. The demon king found himself looking death in the face. An instant later, he lay dead.

Just for a moment, everyone glimpsed Krishna's true self. They saw him as the god Vishnu, wearing flowing, yellow robes, garlanded with sweet-smelling lotus blossoms, and seated on a shining throne. Once again, good had triumphed over evil. How the people of the city sang and celebrated!

THE BIRTH OF BUDDHA

One night a long time ago, the Queen of Nepal had a wonderful dream. She dreamed that beautiful angels carried her away to a heavenly, golden palace, high on a snowy mountaintop. She was bathed in perfumed waters and given a bed of silk. Through the silvery blue moonlight, an ice-white elephant brought her a perfect lotus flower. Sweet music rippled through her head, and trees all around burst into blossom.

When the queen woke, she hurried to tell her husband all about her fabulous dream.

"It felt real!" she insisted.

The amazed king summoned his oldest, wisest adviser to tell them what the dream meant.

"You will have a son," the chief adviser announced. "After he sees old age, disease, and death, he will leave your kingdom to seek true happiness—or enlightenment. He will become a great leader."

Before long the queen did indeed give birth to a baby boy. The king and queen were overjoyed. They called their son Siddhartha.

However, when the prince was only seven days old, the queen died. The king was heartbroken, but he carried on for the sake of his son. He had to bring up Prince Siddhartha on his own.

Siddhartha was a good-natured, loving child, and he made the king happy again. The king loved his son more than life itself and gave him every comfort, surrounding him with beautiful treasures. He hoped that if the prince had everything he could possibly want, he would never go out of the palace. The king couldn't bear the thought of his son leaving him, as the wise old adviser had foreseen.

Siddhartha lived a contented life inside the palace for many years. As he grew older, he began to grow more and more curious about what lay on the other side of the palace walls. The king realized sadly that he couldn't keep the prince in his beautiful prison forever.

"My son," the king sighed at last, "if it will make you happy, I will allow you to go for a chariot ride through our kingdom tomorrow."

Prince Siddhartha couldn't wait, but the king was extremely worried. He had always strictly forbidden anyone to tell the prince about sad, ugly things such as old age, poverty, illness, and death. Of course, the prince had never seen these things inside the palace.

Siddhartha knew nothing about the suffering that existed in the outside world, so the king sent a strict order through his kingdom: "Tomorrow, anyone who is poor, elderly, ill, or dying must stay indoors, out of sight!"

Next morning, the anxious king watched his excited son climb into the royal chariot. The charioteer took up the reins, the palace gates swung open, and Siddhartha's adventure began....

The prince's eyes nearly popped out of his head. There were so many different types of clothes and houses and plants and animals and birds! His ears rang with a thousand new sounds, and his nose twitched with a thousand new smells. Then Siddhartha's eyes fell on the most extraordinary sight of all—a bent-over creature with wrinkled skin and white hair. It moved very slowly and awkwardly, with a funny, wheezing sound.

"Whatever is that animal?" gasped the prince.

"It's not an animal, it's a man," the charioteer replied. He told the prince all about old age. Siddhartha was deeply shocked.

A little further along the road, the prince saw a man lying curled up on the ground. He was making an awful noise and clutching his stomach.

"What on earth is he doing?" cried Siddhartha.

"He is ill and in pain," the charioteer explained, and he told Siddhartha all about disease.

"There can be nothing worse than old age and illness," decided Siddhartha unhappily.

Just then he saw a group of people gathered around a stretcher. On the stretcher lay a woman who was pale, stiff, and still. Water was pouring from the onlookers' eyes, and they were tearing at their hair and clothes.

"That is death," the charioteer whispered, and he explained all about the circle of life. Siddhartha's heart was flooded with an awful new feeling. It was sadness.

The prince was silent and thoughtful as the chariot rumbled along. He realized with horror that his life in the palace had been a lie. He knew he could never go back to living that way. He didn't think he'd ever be happy again, now that he knew there was so much misery in the world.

Suddenly Siddhartha saw a man sitting very still at the side of the road. The man was dressed in a simple robe, and there was a bowl on the ground in front of him. Every now and then, passers-by would stop and bow to the man, then place a few coins or some food into the bowl.

"Stop!" Siddhartha cried to the charioteer. The prince jumped to the ground and hurried over to the strange man. "Who are you, and what are you doing?" Siddhartha asked.

"I am a holy man called a yogi," came the reply. "I have given up all earthly comforts. In this way, I have found freedom from the sadness of this world. I am at peace, and I look forward to happiness in the life after death."

No one ever really knew how Prince Siddhartha came to see the old man, the sick man, the dead woman, and the yogi. Some said they were people who hadn't obeyed the king. Others said that it was the work of the gods. Whatever the case, it was then that the prophecy about Siddhartha came true. The prince left his father's palace and went wandering through the world until he discovered true happiness, or enlightenment. He became known as Buddha, and many millions of people all over the world follow his teachings.

THE TALE OF GURU NANAK

Over five hundred years ago, in a tiny village in northern India, a baby boy was born to an ordinary man and his wife. They called the child Nanak. Many friends and relations came to congratulate the parents and coo over their new son. The man and his wife were surprised to find that there were some visitors they didn't recognize. Holy men and heroes had come from far and wide to see their baby! Some people even said that gods came too. The wise strangers announced that Nanak would one day become a very great man.

Of course, the man and his wife were totally amazed. When all the fuss had died down and everyone had gone home, they decided that the best thing to do was ignore what the strangers had said and carry on normally. They did their best to bring up their son just like all the other village children.

As time went on, the man and his wife couldn't ignore the fact that Nanak did seem to be different. He didn't run around playing noisy games like the other children, but preferred to wander quietly on his own, deep in thought.

By the time Nanak was a young man, he liked nothing better than to sit and talk all day with holy men from the Hindu and Muslim faiths. Nanak would ask them all kinds of thoughtful questions and share his belief that there was only one true God, not many gods. The young man was often so wrapped up in deep thought that he forgot to eat for days on end. He began to look pale and ill. Sometimes he was so lost in his ideas that he would fall over and just lie there in the dirt, thinking.

The man and his wife grew more and more anxious about their son's odd behavior. The most worrying thing was that he didn't have a job, or show any sign of wanting one! The man had hoped that Nanak would follow in his footsteps and work in an office, or even on the family farm, but Nanak just wanted to spend his time thinking and praying.

One day when Nanak was out, the man was worried to see the chief of the village rushing up to the house.

"Come quickly!" the chief ordered, and led the man to a tree at the edge of the village. There was Nanak, fast asleep under the leafy branches.

"What's the problem?" began the puzzled man. "It's only my son asleep—" He broke off and gasped. "—in the shade!" he finished, turning pale.

It was noon and the sun was high overhead. There were several trees around, and none of them was casting a shadow. Yet Nanak's tree was throwing a large patch of shade over him, to keep him cool and comfortable!

After that, the man knew for sure that Nanak was special to God and that he was protected by nature. The man and his wife weren't surprised when Nanak left home to become a guru, or holy teacher.

Guru Nanak impressed everyone with his simple preaching, and crowds of men and women began to follow him. One morning, when Guru Nanak was bathing in the river, his followers saw him disappear under the water—and he didn't come out! There wasn't a bubble. There wasn't a ripple. Guru Nanak had simply vanished. Many followers decided that he must have drowned.

Several days later, Guru Nanak came walking out of the river. Nanak explained to his amazed followers that he had been with God himself, and that all his questions about religion had been answered. There was to be no Hindu or Muslim faith anymore, for everyone was welcome to follow his teachings instead.

The guru lived a very strict life, and his followers sometimes found it difficult to keep to his rules. Once, Nanak was traveling with a follower called Mardana.

They had been on the road for days, and although the guru didn't seem to need food or water, Mardana was starving and thirsty. Mardana was about to faint from hunger, so Nanak allowed him to eat some berries from a nearby bush. Nanak warned Mardana not to save any of the delicious fruit for later, but the foolish follower couldn't resist and secretly filled his pockets with berries.

Later, Mardana began to nibble the berries, and all at once he fell down, stone dead. The guru was shocked and demanded to know what had happened. Mardana's lifeless body magically spoke and explained everything.

"Those berries were poisonous," Guru Nanak cried. "I could only protect you when I knew you were eating them!" But Nanak took pity on his follower. He said a special prayer and brought Mardana back to life.

Guru Nanak's fame soon spread far and wide, though not everyone showed him respect. In one village, where he asked for a bed for the night, everyone was too selfish to help. The only person who offered the holy man lodgings was a poor carpenter who lived in a tiny hut.

"I don't have much, but what I do have is yours," the carpenter generously offered. He insisted on giving the guru his own bed for the night, while he slept on the cold earth floor instead.

The following day, when the carpenter was at work, Guru Nanak took a piece of wood and smashed the man's bed into a thousand pieces, leaving only the four splintered legs sticking up out of the earth. He then went on his way without a word of thanks. The carpenter was horrified when he came home, but as he sadly dug up the remains of his broken bed, he found four pots of treasure buried underneath!

The holy man worked miracles like these all his life and helped many people. When he died, at the age of 70, his body mysteriously disappeared before anyone could bury it. Many people still follow Guru Nanak's teachings today. These followers are called Sikhs.

Sarvar and His Stepbrothers

Sarvar and his three stepbrothers lived on a tiny farm where nothing much ever grew. Despite being poor, Sarvar was a happy, generous, young man. His three stepbrothers were discontented and spiteful. All the same, Sarvar loved them. He was the kind of person who didn't think badly of anybody. On the other hand, the three brothers didn't like Sarvar at all. They couldn't bear to see his sunny smile or hear his cheerful voice.

One day, Sarvar heard that his grandfather had died and left him a huge piece of land to farm. Although Sarvar was sad about his grandfather, he was happy about the new land.

"You'll come and share my land, won't you?" he kindly invited his three stepbrothers. Of course they were only too willing to take some of Sarvar's good fortune.

When the greedy stepbrothers saw the land, they took the best pieces for themselves and left Sarvar with a rocky patch of waste ground for his share. Sarvar didn't complain. Every morning, he would get up cheerfully, pray to God, and then go out to work.

"Praying won't do any good with a useless bit of land like that!" the three stepbrothers snickered behind his back. "It would take a miracle for anything other than weeds to grow there!"

But a miracle is exactly what happened. At harvest time, Sarvar reaped a crop ten times bigger than that of his stepbrothers.

"You haven't as much grain as I have," the concerned Sarvar noticed. "Take whatever you need from my store."

The jealous brothers didn't need to be told twice. That night, they emptied Sarvar's store of all the grain except one sack. Sarvar didn't seem to mind. He gave away his last sack to feed poor and sick people, then lived off the few scraps he could find. Strangely, he seemed to be happier than when his storehouse was full to bursting!

Not long afterward, Sarvar and his stepbrothers had a message from the district governor. They had to go to the city to pay taxes on their land. The mean stepbrothers had no intention of paying any part of the bill. Instead, they worked out a wicked plan.

The stepbrothers told Sarvar that they were taking a trip to the city and asked him if he would like to go too. Sarvar cheerfully accepted, and the brothers set off.

As soon as they were in the city, the brothers said,

"Don't forget to pay your tax bill while you're here, Sarvar. Because it is *your* tax bill, not ours. You own the farm. We just help you out on it."

Sarvar wasn't angry with his double-crossing stepbrothers. Instead, he was worried about embarrassing them because he had given away all his money and couldn't pay the bill. Sarvar fell to his knees in the middle of the busy town square. He began to pray to God that he might not bring shame on his family. Passers-by stopped and wondered at the strange man. By the time Sarvar opened his eyes, quite a crowd had gathered.

The district governor himself had noticed Sarvar. He wanted to know if Sarvar was as holy as he looked. He decided to use a trick to find out. Holy men were usually offered food and drink, so the district governor told a guard to take Sarvar a tray with a bowl and pitcher covered by a cloth. The bowl and pitcher were to be empty.

The guard handed Sarvar the tray, wondering what the holy man would say when he saw the empty bowl and pitcher. When Sarvar blessed the tray and removed the cloth, the guard was astonished to see the bowl filled with rice and the pitcher brimming with milk. He hurried back to the district governor with the news.

"I would like to meet this saint for myself!" the governor cried.

When the three stepbrothers saw that Sarvar was being taken to the district governor, they nearly danced with glee.

"At last!" they thought. "Sarvar is in trouble for once!"

In fact the district governor gave the holy man presents of one hundred thousand gold coins, a fine horse, and a robe made of priceless cloth.

The jealous stepbrothers decided to take drastic action. They plotted to kill Sarvar and steal his expensive gifts. Luckily, the district governor heard about their plan just in time and had the wicked stepbrothers thrown into jail. Even then, Sarvar forgave them. He asked for forgiveness for all the other prisoners, too.

"If Sarvar wants the prisoners released, then they shall be released," ruled the district governor. These criminals were so grateful that they made up their minds to try to follow Sarvar's example and live good lives.

Sarvar was horrified by the starving beggars, ragged children, and sick people he saw in the huge city. He gave away his hundred thousand coins, his fine horse, and his priceless robe to help the poor and needy. He had never felt comfortable with such rich belongings.

The delighted stepbrothers saw a perfect way to ruin Sarvar's reputation once and for all. They went straight to the district governor and told him how Sarvar had insulted him by giving away his gifts. How foolish the stepbrothers looked when Sarvar came riding through the streets on the fine horse, wearing the priceless robe, and carrying the sacks of coins. God had returned the gifts to him!

From that moment on, God made sure that Sarvar was rich, so he could always help those in need. And the evil stepbrothers had what they deserved, too—they stayed poor and unhappy for the rest of their lives.

Two Elephant Tales

There were once five friends who had been blind from birth. Every day, for as long as they could remember, they met each other under the same shady palm tree by the river. As children, they had tried to beat each other at games that didn't need sight, such as wrestling. Now they were old men, with only the energy to sit and chat, so the friends tried to outdo each other in conversation instead.

If one said his brother had been chased by a crocodile, another would say *his* brother had not just been chased by a crocodile, but eaten up! If one said he knew how many grains of sand were on the beach, another said *he* knew how many stars were in the sky. Every day the blind, old men would lie and boast to their hearts' content.

One morning, the five friends were sitting under the palm tree as usual when they sensed that something had quietly joined them. One man heaved himself to his feet, stretched out his arms, and felt his hands hit something rough and flat and wide.

"It's a huge wall!" he cried.

"How could someone have built a wall without our hearing?" laughed another friend. He pushed himself up and put out his hands.

"I can feel two long, sharp spears!" he cried.

Another blind man stood up and felt in front of him.

"I don't know what either of you is talking about!" he laughed. "I'm holding a ragged piece of rope!"

"No!" cried the fourth blind man, who was also now on his feet. "I've wrapped my arms around something that's tall and round and sturdy. It's a tree trunk."

"Stop it, all of you!" sighed the fifth blind man, as he straightened up with a creak. "I'll tell you what it is." He stretched out his hands and grabbed something that was long and swaying from side to side.

"AAARGH!" he screamed. "It's a snake!"

Suddenly the air was filled with laughter.

"You foolish old men!" came the voice of a little boy from nearby. "It's not a wall, or a pair of spears, or a piece of rope, or a tree trunk, or a snake . . . it's an ELEPHANT!"

The first friend stopped patting the elephant's side. The second friend slowly moved away from the elephant's tusks. The third friend quickly let go of the elephant's tail. The fourth friend gently took his arms from around the elephant's leg. The fifth friend dropped the elephant's trunk.

The blind old men began to back away carefully. They had obviously felt the elephant while he was in a patient mood. They didn't want to stick around to find out what he felt like when he was angry!

After that, the five friends still went every day to the shady palm tree by the river, but they were a little more thoughtful and a little less boastful than before. They had realized that it is best to learn the truth directly from one who knows it.

The courtiers at Emperor Akbar's palace were once taught a lesson by an elephant, too. Emperor Akbar had a wonderful chief minister. He was thoughtful and careful and sensible and very, very wise. The other courtiers were extremely jealous of him. They ran around all day, doing things. They got hot and bothered and tired, while the chief minister just sat next to Emperor Akbar and *thought* all day. The courtiers couldn't understand why he was paid for just thinking!

One day, Emperor Akbar decided to put a stop to the courtiers' mumbling and grumbling and moaning and groaning. He pulled aside a curtain to reveal a huge elephant dressed in royal finery.

"Whoever can tell me the weight of this animal will be my next chief minister!" Emperor Akbar announced.

The courtiers gasped and scratched their heads. For a whole week, they tried to think of different ways to weigh the elephant. Some tried doing complicated sums—but they didn't have enough fingers and toes to count on. Others tried building elephant-sized weighing scales—but they couldn't make them big enough. One courtier even suggested chopping up the elephant and weighing each piece! (As you can imagine, no one thought much of *that* idea.)

"Can no one tell me the weight of the royal elephant?" Emperor Akbar asked at the end of the week. The courtiers hung their heads in shame.

"I can," said the chief minister, and he calmly gave the correct answer.

Emperor Akbar grinned from ear to ear.

"Well done!" he beamed. "Tell them how you did it."

"I took the elephant to the river and put it in a boat," the chief minister began. "I marked where the water came up to on the side of the boat. Next I took the elephant out and began to fill the boat with sacks of wheat. I stopped filling the boat when it had sunk down into the water as far as the mark I had made.

"After that I counted how many sacks of wheat I had used. I knew that the weight of the sacks of wheat must be the same as the weight of the elephant. I just weighed one sack of wheat and multiplied that by the number of sacks I had used and I found—"

"The weight of the elephant!" Emperor Akbar finished, triumphantly. "A wise person is he who gets things done with the least fuss," he announced—and all the astonished courtiers had to agree!

INDEX